Project 7-11

Exploring
Maths

Book 1

Jim Boucher and George Rodda

for 10-11 year olds

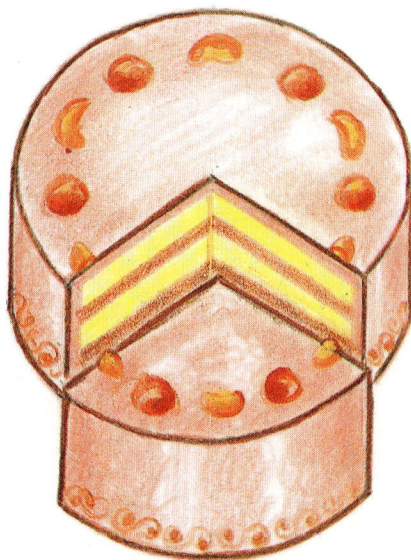

Letts

May likes to do curved stitching and uses coloured threads. She was showing Mary how she got her designs with pencil first.

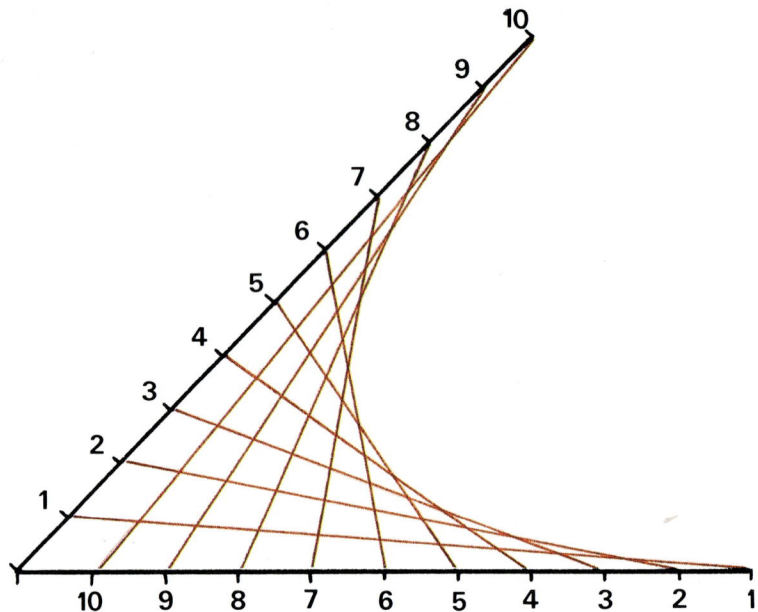

▶ Can you name this curve?

_____

After Mary had done a curve with one angle and two arms she wanted to do a design from four arms.

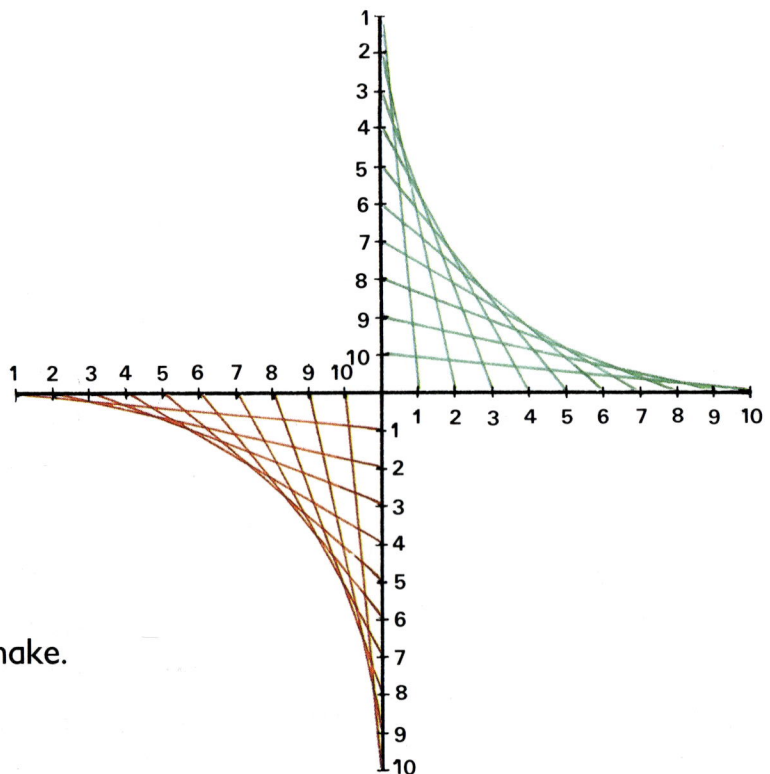

Mary still has two curves to make.

▶ Finish the design for her.

▶ What angles are these?

_____

May then started this design.

▶ Finish it for her.

▶ How many angles are used altogether? How many arms?

_____ angles

_____ arms

I've drawn you this outline for a yacht. Can you complete it?

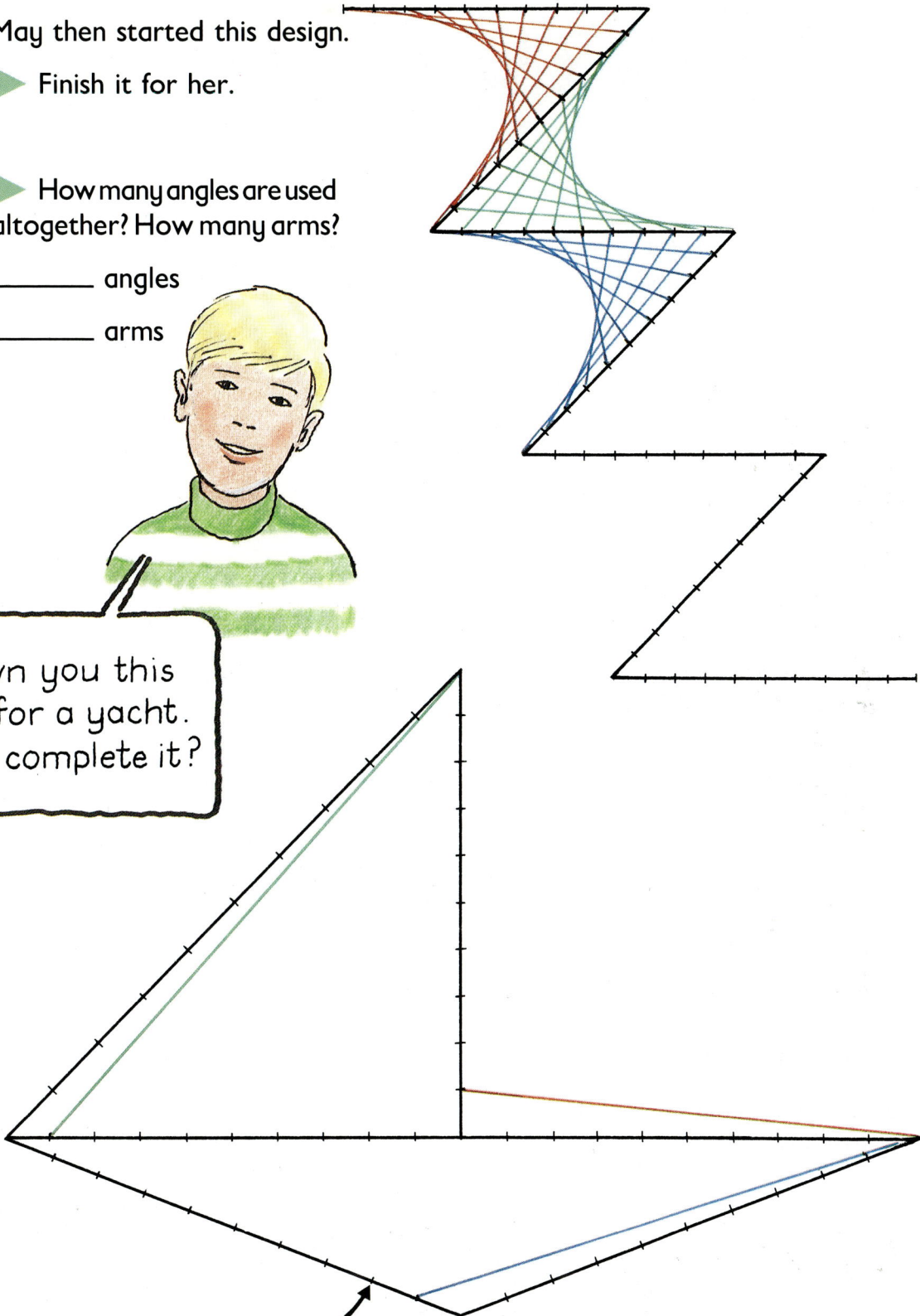

Start here

I'm going to do some designs in coloured threads. Why don't you try some?

2 On the level

Mr Level used a spirit level when he built this house.

glass with bubble

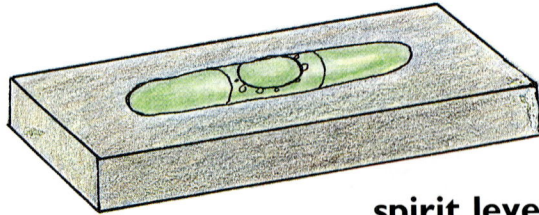

spirit level

Mr Slipshod didn't use one.

I can make a spirit level.

bubble

water

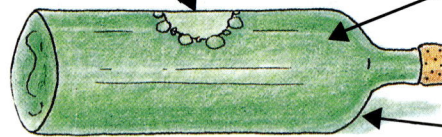

bottle

▶ Make a spirit level like Ian's. Leave a bubble of air in the bottle.

Ian used his spirit level to check if these things were level or **horizontal**.

a table top

the floor

the draining board

▶ Which one should not be horizontal? _____

▶ Use your spirit level to find more things which are horizontal.

Mr Level uses a plumb line to test that his walls are upright and **vertical**.

I have made this plumb line using a piece of string and a weight.

▶ Make a plumb line like Ruth's and test these things to see if they are vertical.

door _____   window _____

I have drawn this picture which has some horizontal and some vertical lines on it.

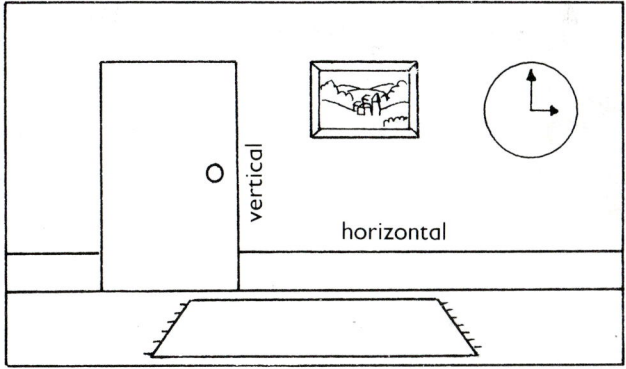

▶ Colour the horizontal lines in red.

▶ Colour the vertical lines in blue.

This spider is coming down to earth.

▶ Is the spider travelling horizontally or vertically?

_____

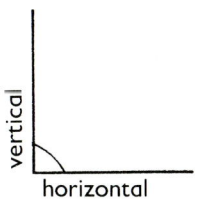

▶ Use a protractor to help you fill in the missing number.

There are _____ degrees between horizontal and vertical.

5

Why did the Romans use the letters M, D, C and L to represent numbers?

Old Roman records have shown that 1000 was written ⊕D so it is believed that the other symbols came from it.

D, half the whole circle, C, and L, half of C.

I think I know now what they stand for.

M represents →	1000
D →	
C →	
L →	

▶ Help Gary with his Roman numerals for large numbers.

CCXV MILES TO LONDON

▶ How far is it to London?

_____ miles

Don't forget that C sometimes comes before M and means 900 (100 less than 1000).

▶ What do these stand for?

| MCMLXX | MCMLXXX | MCMXC | MCMXI |

_____   _____   _____   _____

Can you write these dates in Roman numerals? 1-9-1066. 25-12-1990.

1 – 9 – 1066

_____

25 – 12 – 1990

_____

MDCXV

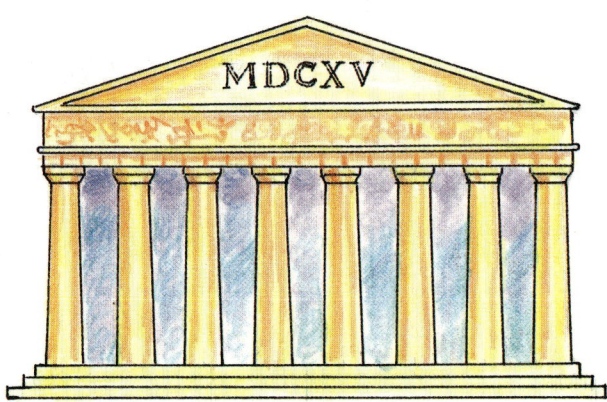

I see Roman numerals quite a lot on T.V.

▶ Can you read the date on this Roman-style building?

_____

▶ When does Leon see these?

_____

_____

4 Fathom it out

▶ Stretch your hand out on a piece of paper.

▶ Mark where the tip of your thumb and the tip of your little finger are.

span

My span is 16 cm.

▶ Now measure your span.

My span is _____ cm.

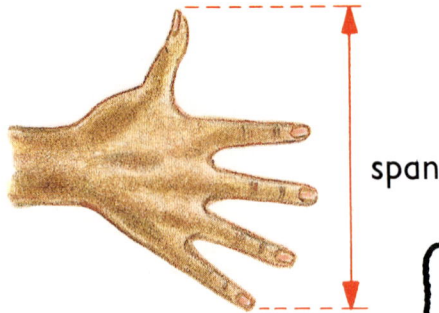

▶ Measure the height of your chair using your span.

The height of my chair is _____ spans.

▶ Change the spans to cm.

The height of my chair is _____ cm.

height

▶ Check the height with a ruler.

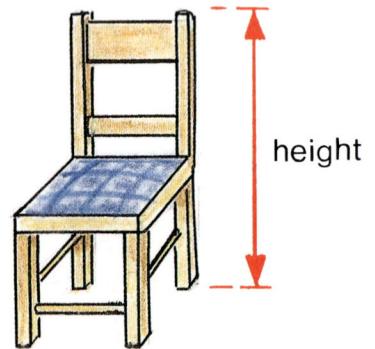

The ancient Egyptians measured in **statures**.

1 stature

1 stature

Which stature, ↔ or ↕, is easier to use when measuring a length of cloth?

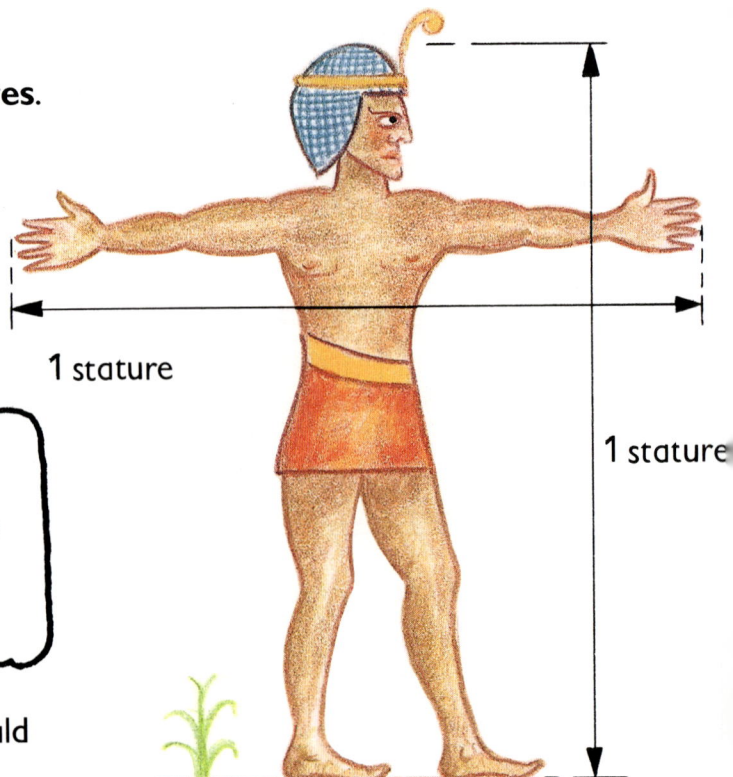

For an <u>adult</u> ancient Egyptian they should both be the same measure.

Make marks on a wall or a floor to help you check your statures.

Finger tip to finger tip, my stature is _____ cm.

Floor to top of head, my stature is _____ cm.

The ancient Egyptians used this rule.

Rule 1
8 spans = 1 stature

▶ See if the rule works for you.

My span is _____ cm.

So 8 spans are _____ cm.

▶ Are 8 of your spans more than, less than, or equal to your stature? _____

I know another rule about statures.

Rule 2
For depth of water:
1 fathom is 1 stature

▶ How many spans deep is your bath?

▶ Is your bath more than, or less than 1 fathom deep? _____

Ancient Egyptians had big hands.

Rule 3
1 span is 24 cm

▶ Fill in the blank spaces in the sum below for an ancient Egyptian.

1 span is 24 cm.

8 spans are _____ cm.

So 1 stature or 1 fathom is nearly _____ metres.

9

5 Scoring with darts

This ring scores **treble**.

This ring scores **double**.

This ring scores 25.

A **bull's-eye** scores 50.

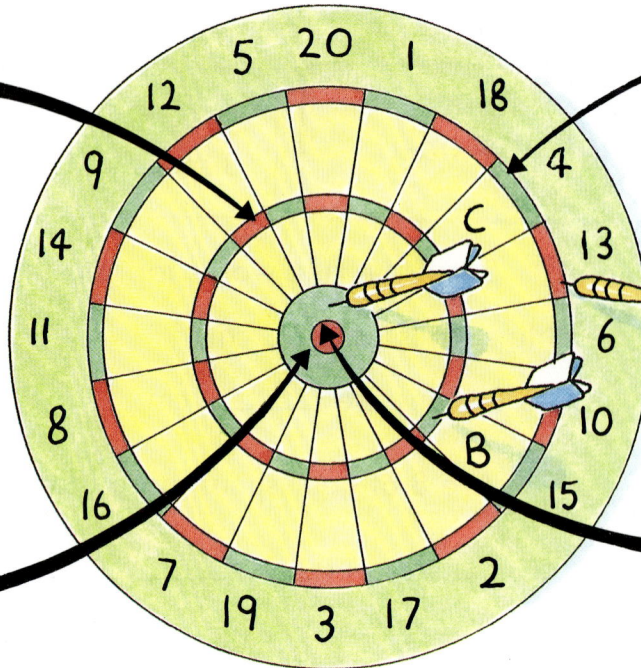

C

A

13

B

Find the total for my darts A, B and C.

dart A		double 13
dart B		treble 15
dart C		inner ring
total		

I once scored:
treble 18,

double 19,

bull's-eye.

total

My maths improved when I began playing darts. You have to be able to add and subtract quickly, as well as double, halve and treble.

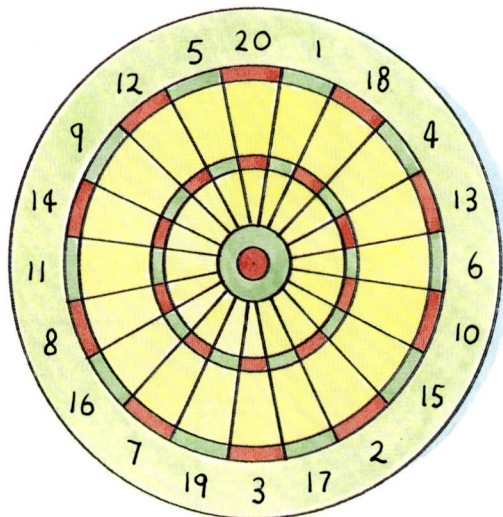

▶ See if you can answer some of Joe's questions on the dartboard.

▶ With only three darts how can you score:

1 100 in 4 different ways? _____

2 the highest possible score? _____

3 the lowest possible score? _____

4 50 – using "doubles" only? _____

5 27 – with the 1st dart scoring a double? _____

6 150 – with the last dart scoring a double? _____

This is the score-board for Joe v Tom.

Joe	Tom
301	301
267	275
195	215
120	115
60	75
5	42
0	

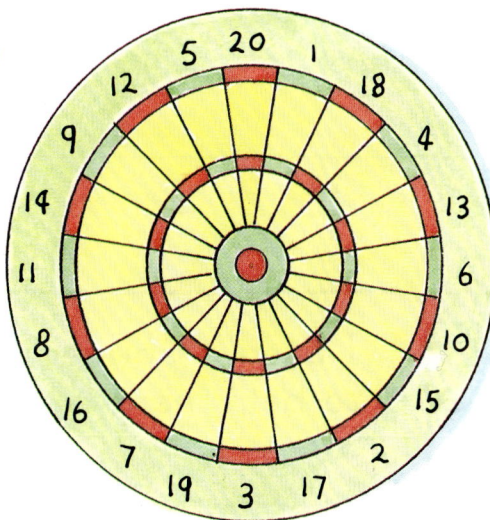

▶ Who won the game? _____

▶ Draw two darts in the board to show how he won with only two darts – finishing on a double.

▶ Is there more than one way? _____

6 Twists and turns

I have drawn round this teacup and then cut out a circle.

▶ Draw round a teacup and cut out a circle like Pat has done.

▶ Fold the circle into two halves.

▶ What is the name of the line which is made by the fold?

D __ __ M __ __ __ R

fold

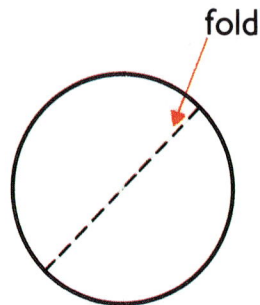

▶ Fold the paper into two halves to make a second crease.

▶ Where is the centre of the circle?

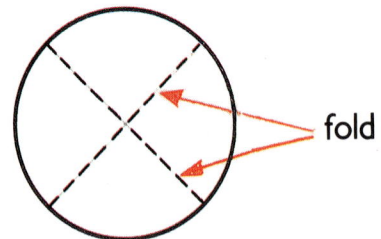

fold

I used a saucer to help me draw a circle.

▶ Draw round a saucer and cut out a new circle.

▶ Write the name **circumference** round the edge of your circle.

I cut out a strip of paper and joined the ends to make a circular loop.

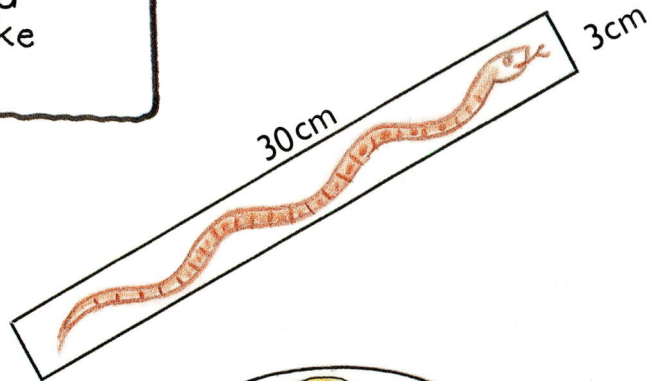

30cm
3cm

▶ Cut out a strip of paper like Mary's.

▶ Draw a red snake on one side and a yellow snake on the other side.

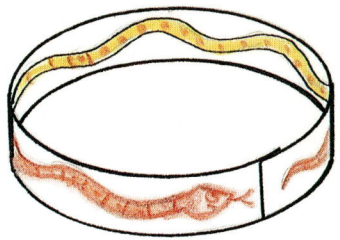

▶ Join the ends to make a circular loop.

▶ Which coloured snake is on the outside of the loop? _____

▶ Which coloured snake is on the inside of the loop? _____

▶ Change them over.

I put <u>one</u> twist in my strip before I joined the ends. Which one of my snakes is on the inside and which one is on the outside?

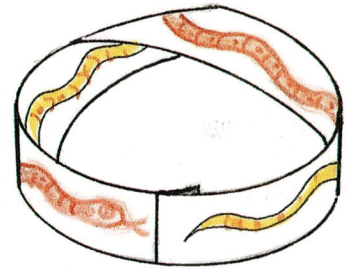

You will be surprised by the answer to Hamid's question.

Make two more loops and I will surprise you again.

Mary's loop   Hamid's loop

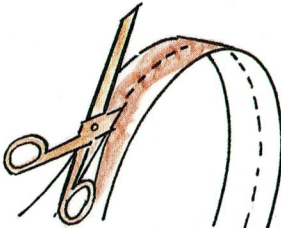
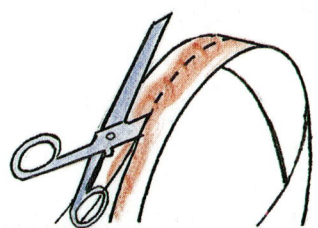

▶ Make one loop like Mary's and one like Hamid's.

▶ Now cut your loops in half lengthways.

▶ Your loop like Mary's becomes two loops.
What happens to your loop like Hamid's? Are you amazed?

13

Tammy has drawn these circles. In the first circle she has put two dots on the circumference and joined them together with a **chord**. She then put 3 dots on the next, and 4, 5, 6 and 7 on each of the others.

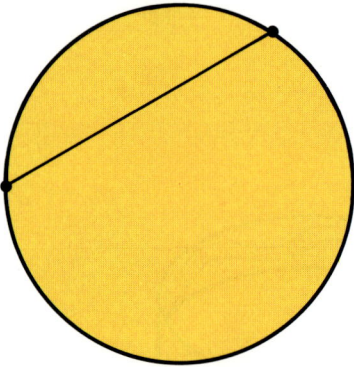

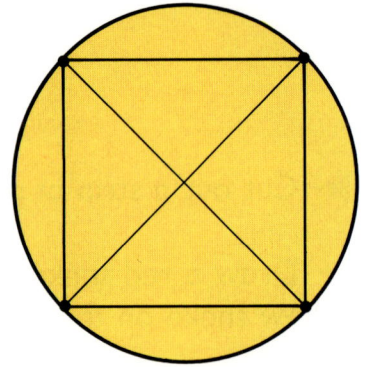

I've done the first three and have started a table.
Make sure that each point is joined to all the others!

Number of points	Number of chords
2	1
3	3
4	
5	
6	
7	
8	

▶ Count the chords in each circle and complete the table.

▶ See if you can spot the pattern to work out the number of chords for 8 dots.

A **diameter** is a special chord.

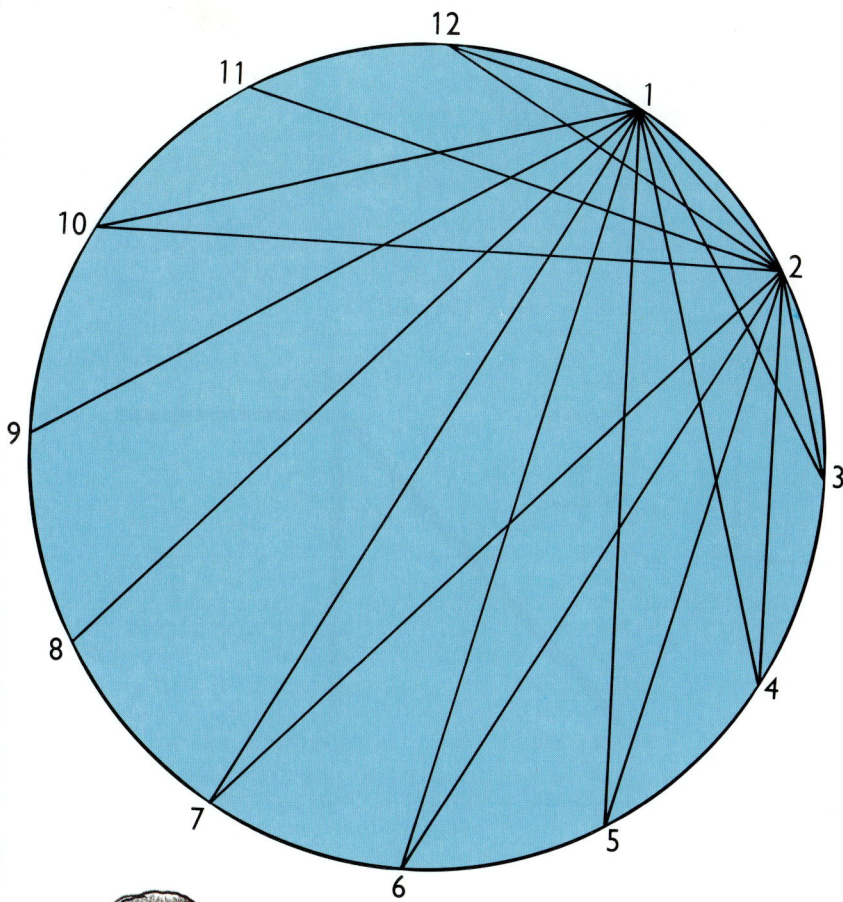

You'll get a super pattern if you join each point to every other point.
I've started it for you.

▶ When you have finished see if you can find the number of chords without counting them!

Ruth has started this pattern. Each number is joined to the number which is twice as big as itself.

For example:
1 ⟶ 2
2 ⟶ 4
3 ⟶ 6
4 ⟶ 8
and so on.

When you get to 13 you will have to join it to 2, because 2 then becomes the 26th point!
So, 14 will be joined to ☐

15 to ☐   16 to ☐   and so on.

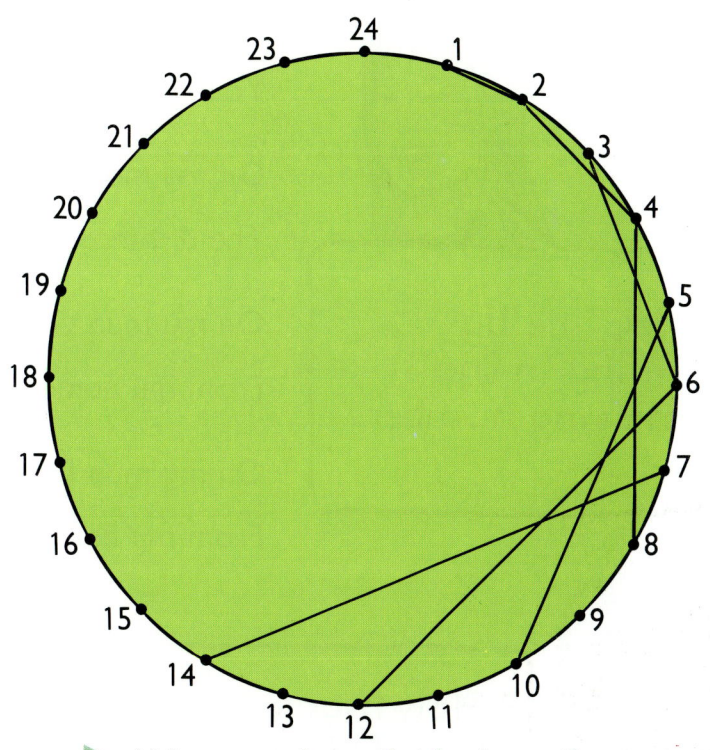

▶ When you have finished see if you can describe the shape you get!

_____

_____

8 Far and away

I've been cycling and have drawn this map.

Scale: 1 cm represents 1 km

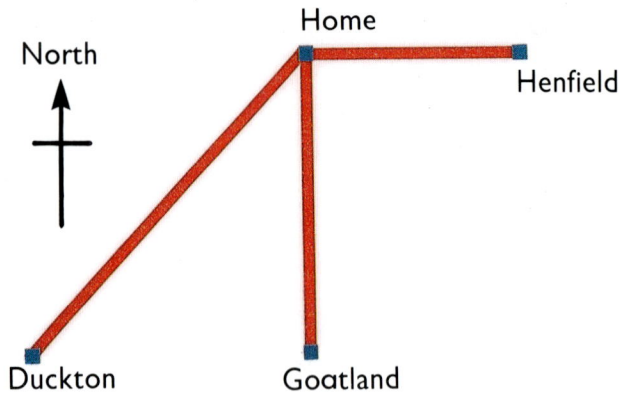

North

Home

Henfield

Duckton

Goatland

▶ Use your set square or protractor to help you write in the missing directions.

Goatland is _____ of May's home.

Henfield is _____ of May's home.

Duckton is _____ of May's home.

Help me by filling in the missing numbers.

You will need a ruler to help May.

On my map it is _____ cm from home to Henfield.

The distance from home to Henfield is _____ km.

On my map Goatland is _____ cm from home.

From my home to Goatland is _____ km.

On my map Duckton is _____ cm from home.

From my home to Duckton is _____ km.

How many km will I cycle to travel this journey?

May's journey

Home to Henfield,
back home,
to Duckton and back.

_____ km

I've found a map which shows the twisty road from Goatland to Henfield.

Scale: 1 cm represents 1 km

Henfield

Goatland

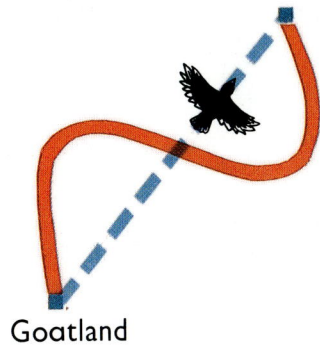

▶ Use a ruler to help you fill in the missing numbers in the following sentences.

As the crow flies it is _____ km from Goatland to Henfield.

▶ Lay a piece of fine chain or string along the twisty road on the map.

▶ Measure the length of the chain or string

The length is _____ cm.

The road distance from Goatland to Henfield is

_____ km.

Scale: 1 cm represents 1 km

Henfield

string or chain

Goatland

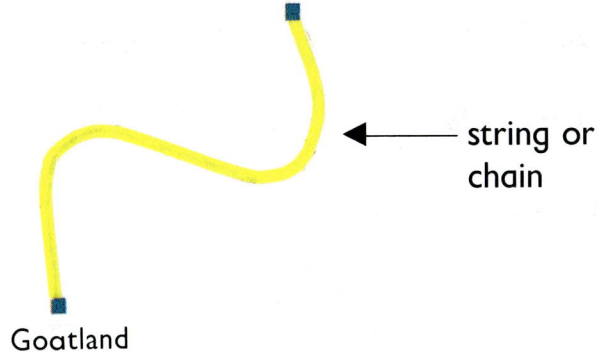

Can you make your own map like I have done?

For example:

A-town

B-town

Your home

C-town

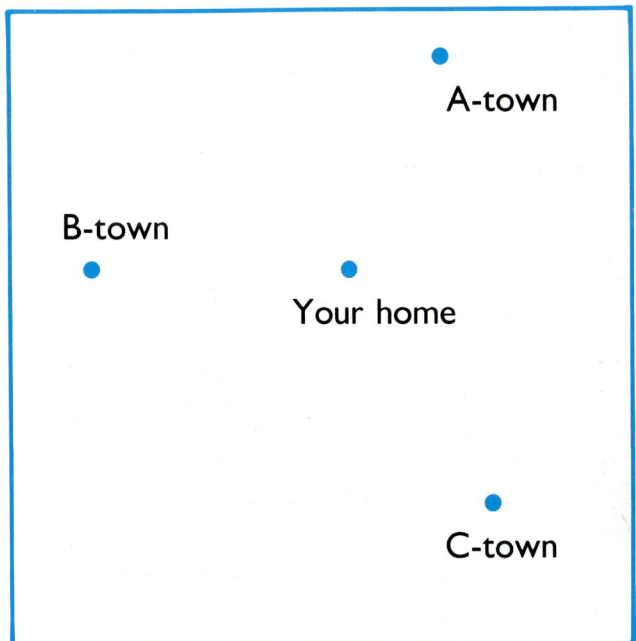

▶ You will need to choose three places near your home and find out:
1 how far away they are, and
2 in which direction they are.

9 A piece of cake

The three of us are going to share this cake.

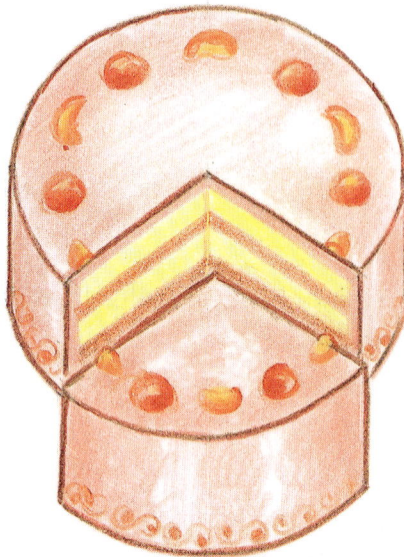

▶ What fraction of the cake will they have each?

_____

Yes, please!

▶ Use your electronic calculator to change these fractions into decimals.

$\frac{1}{4}$ → 1 ÷ 4 →

$\frac{1}{4}$ is exactly 0.25. Which of the other fractions can be shown as exact decimals?

Fraction	Decimal
$\frac{1}{4}$	0.25
$\frac{1}{2}$	0.5
$\frac{1}{3}$	
$\frac{2}{3}$	0.6666666
$\frac{3}{4}$	
$\frac{1}{7}$	
$\frac{2}{7}$	0.2857142
$\frac{3}{7}$	

_____

_____

I am working out $\frac{3}{7}$ as a decimal without a calculator. When can I stop?

$\frac{3}{7} = 3 \div 7$
$= 0.4285714285714.$

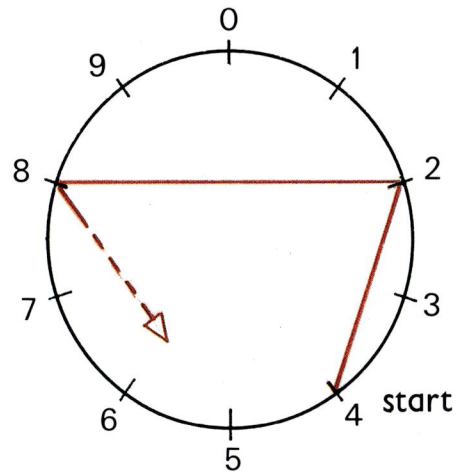

▶ Follow May's decimal round this circle by joining:

$4 \rightarrow 2 \rightarrow 8 \rightarrow \ldots$

I have found some patterns with my fractions.

Pat folded a circle of paper into eight parts.
She was thinking about ⅜ so she joined every third point.

▶ Finish off Pat's pattern. It makes a lovely star.

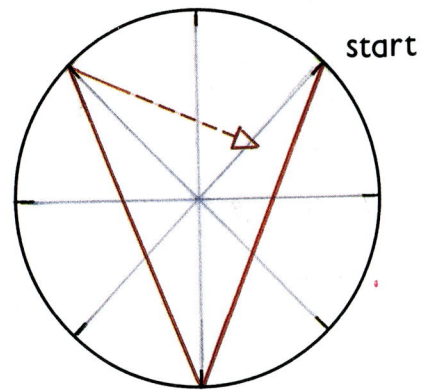

I have started a new pattern for $\frac{1}{4}$ which is the same as $\frac{2}{8}$.
I had to start at two places to finish this pattern.

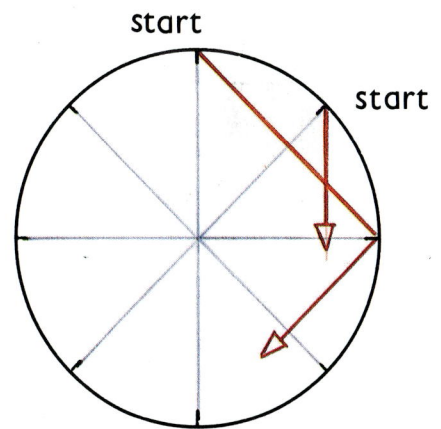

▶ Finish off Pat's pattern and then try some more for yourself.

▶ Try $\frac{1}{6}, \frac{2}{6}, \frac{3}{6}, \frac{4}{6}, \frac{5}{6}.$

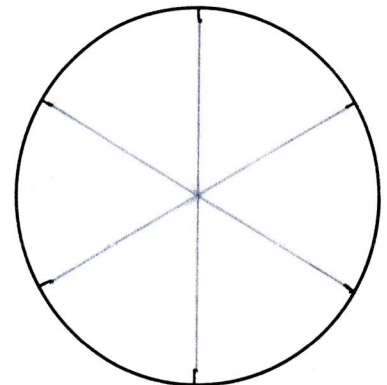

I know of some interesting multiplication sums. I've done the first two for you.

$$\begin{array}{r} 37 \\ \times\ 3 \\ \hline 111 \end{array}$$

$$\begin{array}{r} 37 \\ \times\ 6 \\ \hline 222 \end{array}$$

▶ See what you can find in these.

$$\begin{array}{r} 37 \\ \times\ 9 \\ \hline \end{array}$$

$$\begin{array}{r} 37 \\ \times\ 12 \\ \hline \end{array}$$

$$\begin{array}{r} 37 \\ \times\ 15 \\ \hline \end{array}$$

$$\begin{array}{r} 37 \\ \times\ 18 \\ \hline \end{array}$$

We are multiplying by a number made up of 3s. Continue until the "magic" disappears.

$$\begin{array}{r} 37 \\ \times\ 21 \\ \hline \end{array}$$

$$\begin{array}{r} 37 \\ \times\ 24 \\ \hline \end{array}$$

$$\begin{array}{r} 37 \\ \times\ 27 \\ \hline \end{array}$$

$$\begin{array}{r} 37 \\ \times\ 30 \\ \hline \end{array}$$

I don't need a calculator to do this, do you?

▶ Now double 37 making 74. Use the same multipliers and keep multiplying until the "magic" disappears.

I know some more "magic" multiplication sums using 9.
See if you can follow the pattern and fill in the missing products.

$$999999 \times 2 = 1999998$$
$$999999 \times 3 = 2999997$$
$$999999 \times 4 = \underline{\hspace{3cm}}$$
$$999999 \times 5 = \underline{\hspace{3cm}}$$
$$999999 \times 6 = 5999994$$
$$999999 \times 7 = \underline{\hspace{3cm}}$$
$$999999 \times 8 = \underline{\hspace{3cm}}$$
$$999999 \times 9 = 8999991$$

You can't do this one on your calculator.

▶ Can you say why?

_____

_____

_____

$$123456789 \times 9 = 111111111$$
$$123456789 \times 18 = 222222222$$
$$123456789 \times 27 =$$
$$123456789 \times 36 =$$
$$123 \ldots \quad \times \quad =$$

Can you complete my pattern for me?

$$9 \times 9 + 7 = 88$$
$$98 \times 9 + 6 =$$
$$987 \times 9 + 5 =$$
$$9876 \times 9 + 4 =$$
$$98765 \times 9 + 3 =$$
$$987654 \times 9 + 2 =$$
$$9876543 \times 9 + 1 =$$
$$98765432 \times 9 + 0 = 888888888$$

11 Reflections

mirror line

Ruth | Яутн

I know what a line of symmetry is. It is like a mirror line.

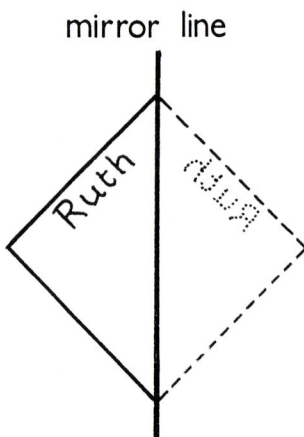

Can you see a square? The reflection of my name looks like Яutн.

▶ Hold a flat mirror on its edge along the mirror line.

Write my name and yours on a square. Now write the reflections of our names.

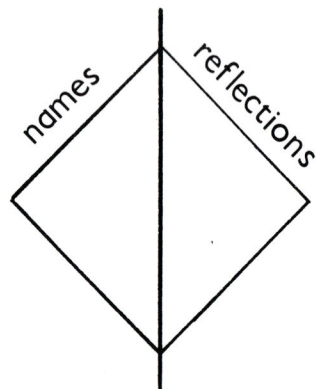

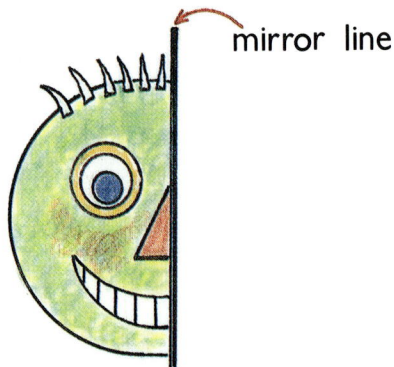

names | reflections

mirror line

Only half of these shapes have been drawn. Finish drawing them.

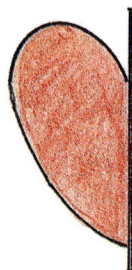

fold

How many lines of symmetry, or mirror lines, does a circle have?

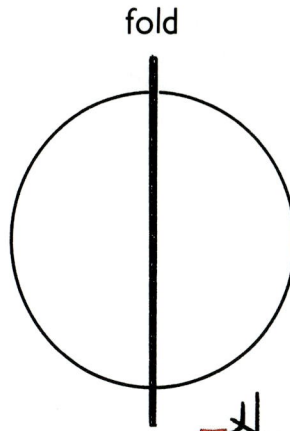

▶ Cut out a circle and try to fold **all** the mirror lines.

Don't be disappointed if you can't fold all of them.

lines of symmetry

Snowflakes have mirror lines of symmetry.

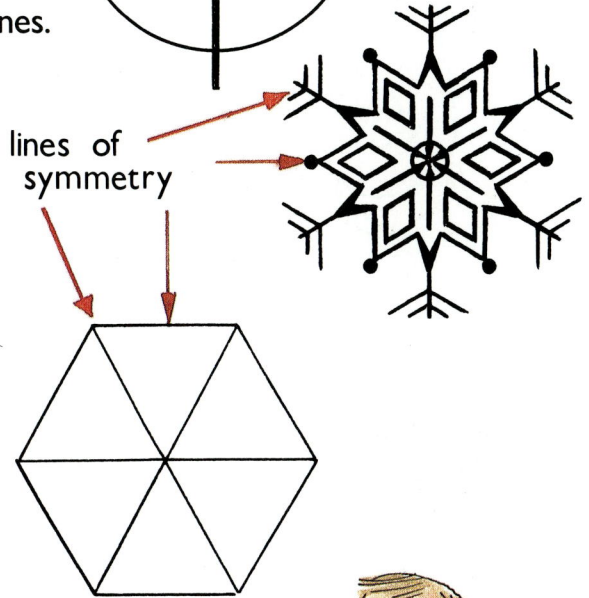

▶ Use a mirror to check that this snowflake and this hexagon each have 6 lines of symmetry.

Use crayons to make your own snowflake patterns on these grids.

Make sure that they have 6 lines of symmetry.

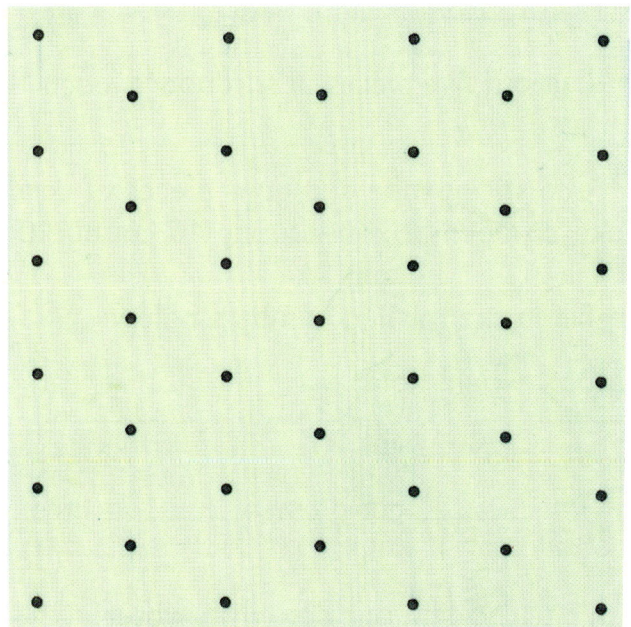

fold

12 Fill it up

My mother uses this measuring jug.

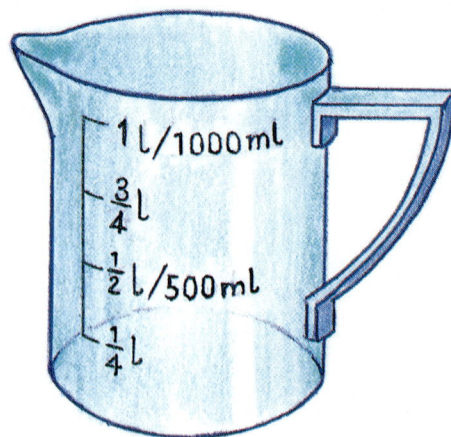

1 l/1000 ml
3/4 l
1/2 l/500 ml
1/4 l

▶ Look carefully at the markings on a measuring jug.

It should show markings for **litres** (l) and **millilitres** (ml).

▶ Fill your jug to the ½ litre mark.

▶ Now pour out water until you only have 250 ml.

Don't forget that 1 millilitre is the same volume as 1 cubic centimetre.

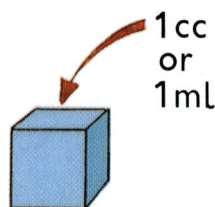

1cc or 1ml

▶ Cut out five pieces of cardboard, each 10 cm by 10 cm.

▶ Use sticky tape and your pieces of card to make an open box measuring 10 cm by 10 cm by 10 cm.

▶ Fill in the missing numbers below.

My box would hold:

_____ cm × _____ cm × _____ cm

= _____ cubic cm = _____ litre.

10cm
10cm
10cm

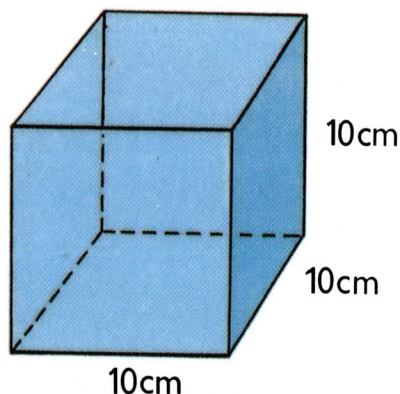

Don't try to fill your box with water!

▶ Use your 10 cm cube to help you work out how many litres of water each of these fish tanks will hold.

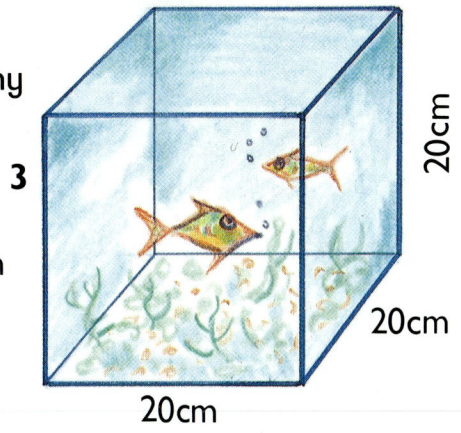

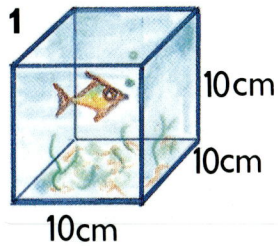

1

10cm
10cm
10cm

_____ **litres**

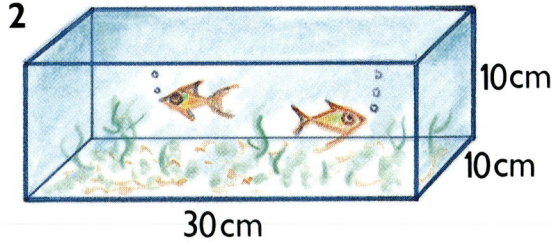

2

10cm
10cm
30cm

_____ **litres**

3

20cm
20cm
20cm

_____ **litres**

▶ Look at your favourite beaker and estimate how many cc or ml it will hold.

? ml

▶ Write down your estimate. _____

▶ Use a measuring jug to check your estimate.

I think this teacup will hold 20 ml.

▶ Check how many ml one of your teacups will hold.

Mary's mother makes lemon squash in this big bottle.

5 litres SQUASH

700 cc

▶ How many small bottles could be filled from 5 litres?

_____

▶ How many ml will be left in the big bottle?

_____

▶ How many glasses could be filled from 5 litres?

_____

25cc

13 Up in smoke

My grandad should stop smoking!

PIPE TOBACCO
25g   £1·40

Smoking is not only bad for your health, but it is very expensive.

Emma's grandad smokes three 25 g packets of tobacco per week.

▶ Help Emma show him how much he could save each year!

He spends per week £1.40 × 3 = £ [　]

He spends per year £ [　] × 52 = £ [　]

▶ How much does it cost Emma's grandad to the nearest £? £ [　]

Tobacco is packed in cartons of 250 g.

I worked out how many kilos and cartons he smoked like this.

My grandad smokes 25 g × 3 = [   ] g per week.

He smokes 25 g × 3 × 52 = [   ] g in 1 year

Does this help?

→ 75 g × 50 = [   ] g

→ 75 g × 2 = [   ] g

▶ Help Emma show her grandad how much tobacco he smokes.

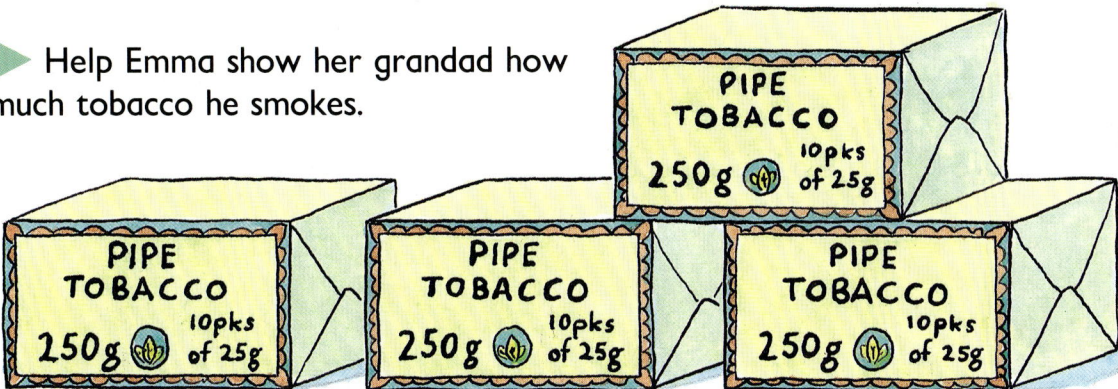

Four cartons hold [   ] kg.

How many cartons and how many kilos does my grandad send up in smoke in one year?

[   ] cartons   [   ] kg

14 Whose turn next?

I will share my bicycle with Ruth and Tom.

If the three children take turns the order could be:

Alan, Ruth and then Tom
or
Ruth, Alan and then Tom.

▶ Using the first initial of each of their names finish this list of all the different orders.

1	A R T	2	R A T	3	T A R
4	A __ __	5	R __ __	6	T __ __

I like wearing hats.

I 　　II 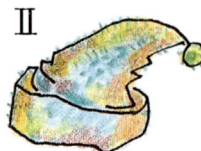　　III

▶ Draw pictures on a separate piece of paper to show the six different orders in which Ruth can wear her three hats.

For example:

| Order 1 |

Day 1 　　Day 2 　　Day 3

Ruth has been given another hat.

IV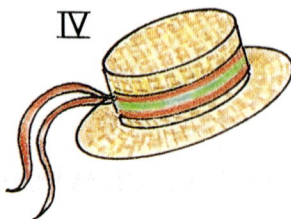

▶ Use numbers to write down the 24 different orders in which Ruth can wear her hats in a table like the one shown.

Order	Day			
	1	2	3	4
1	I	II	III	IV
2	I	II	IV	III
3	II	I	III	IV
4				
5				
6				

Can you work out the number of my house? It is made up from a 1, a 2, and a 3.

2 **1** **3**

▶ Finish writing all the possible numbers for Tom's house.

My house number is an even number.

Possible numbers for Tom's house:

1	2	3
1		2
2	1	3
	3	1

▶ Which two numbers could be right? _____ and _____

I know which number it is. It will divide exactly by 8.

▶ Now write down the number of Tom's house.

_____

I can choose a cake from this plate of four.

▶ In how many ways can Alan choose:

1 his first cake? **3** his third cake?
2 his second cake? **4** his fourth cake?

▶ Are there 24 different orders in which Alan can eat the four cakes?

Use these four number cards to make up the sum with the largest possible answer.

1 **2** **3** **4**

☐ ☐ x ☐ ☐ = ☐

15 Fraction families

1	2	3	4	5	6	7	8	9	10	←
2	4	6	8	10	12	14	16	18	20	←
3	6	9	12	15	18	21	24	27	30	
4	8	12	16	20	24	28	32	36	40	
5	10	15	20	25	30	35	40	45	50	
6	12	18	24	30	36	42	48	54	60	
7	14	21	28	35	42	49	56	63	70	
8	16	24	32	40	48	56	64	72	80	
9	18	27	36	45	54	63	72	81	90	
10	20	30	40	50	60	70	80	90	100	

If you look at the top two rows of my multiplication square you will see $\frac{1}{2}$, $\frac{2}{4}$, $\frac{3}{6}$, $\frac{4}{8}$, and so on.
They all belong to the $\frac{1}{2}$ family.

Look at the second and fourth row.

$\frac{2}{4}$, $\frac{4}{8}$, $\frac{6}{12}$, $\frac{\square}{\square}$, $\frac{\square}{\square}$, $\frac{\square}{\square}$, $\frac{\square}{\square}$, $\frac{\square}{\square}$, $\frac{\square}{\square}$, $\frac{\square}{\square}$

To which family do these all belong?

_____

▶ Complete these fraction families:

$\frac{1}{3}$ $\square$ $\square$ $\square$ $\square$ $\square$ $\square$ $\square$ $\square$ $\square$

$\frac{1}{5}$ $\square$ $\square$ $\square$ $\square$ $\square$ $\square$ $\square$ $\square$ $\square$

$\frac{1}{10}$ $\square$ $\square$ $\square$ $\square$ $\square$ $\square$ $\square$ $\square$ $\square$

 0·

 0·

I want you to tell me what <u>decimal</u> fraction of a £ these coins are.

 0·

 0·

 0·

Can you "match" the following fractions? I've done one for you.

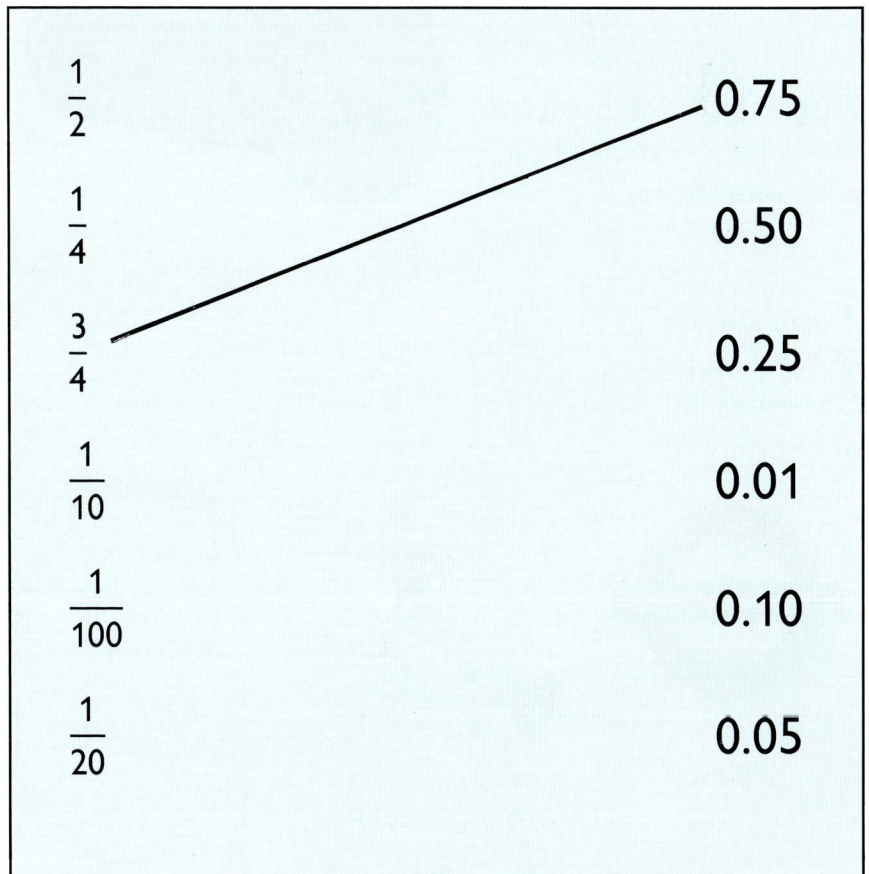

$\frac{1}{2}$ 0.75

$\frac{1}{4}$ 0.50

$\frac{3}{4}$ 0.25

$\frac{1}{10}$ 0.01

$\frac{1}{100}$ 0.10

$\frac{1}{20}$ 0.05

Keep your pencil on the paper

Try tracing over these shapes with a pencil without lifting it from the paper. You mustn't go over any line twice!

A

B

C

We call these **networks**.

D

E

If you can trace a network according to the rules it is **traversable**.

This is a map of the London Underground network.

UNDERGROUND

I have to ride my horse round this course without going over any path twice.
Can I do it?

F

Notice that the course has three junctions where an even number of paths meet and only two where an odd number of paths meet.

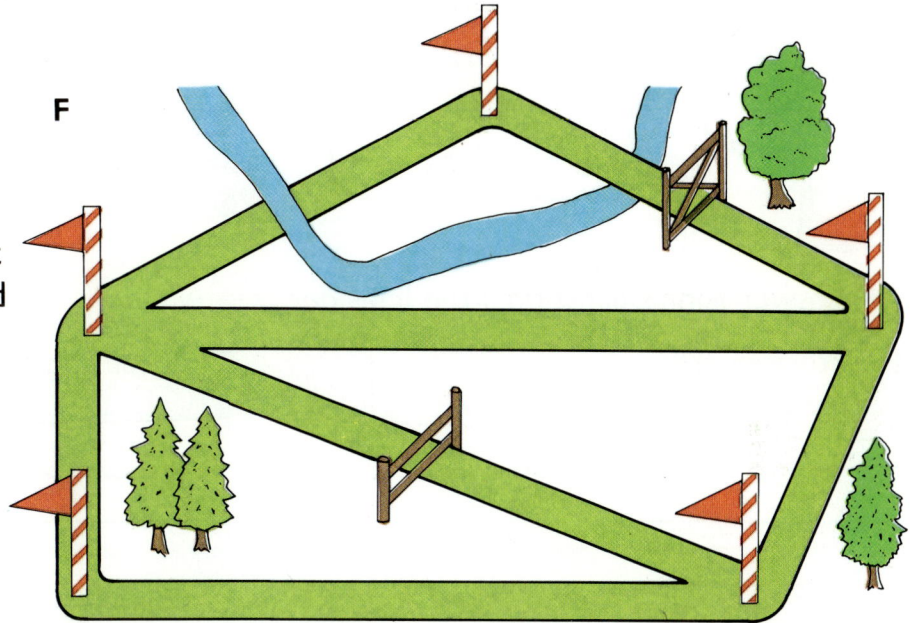

Network	Number of even junctions	Number of odd junctions	Is the network traversable?
A	1	4	no
B			
C			
D			
E			
F			

▶ Fill in this table for the networks on these pages. Pat has done the first for you.

▶ Can you find the rule for deciding if a network is traversable or not?

_____

_____

These railway lines always stay the same distance apart.

What would happen if they didn't?

▶ Answer Alan's question if the lines get:

1 further apart.

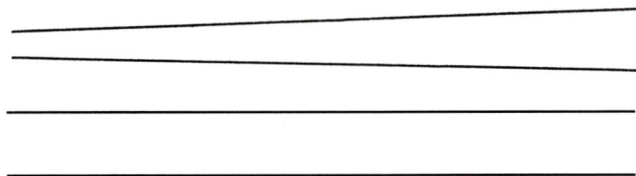

2 closer together.

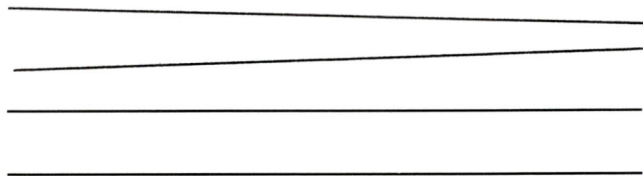

Railway lines are **parallel** lines.

1 The top and bottom edges of this page are parallel.

Their distance apart is _____ cm.

2 The side edges of this page are parallel.

Their distance apart is _____ cm.

I can find lots of parallel lines on this matchbox.

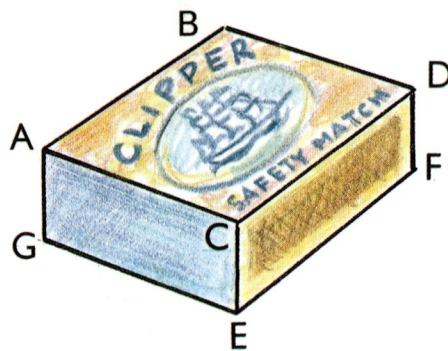

▶ On a matchbox, measure the distance between parallel edges, like AB and CD.

▶ Did you measure the distance between lines AB and EF?

They are **parallel**.

I have discovered how to make AC and BD further apart.

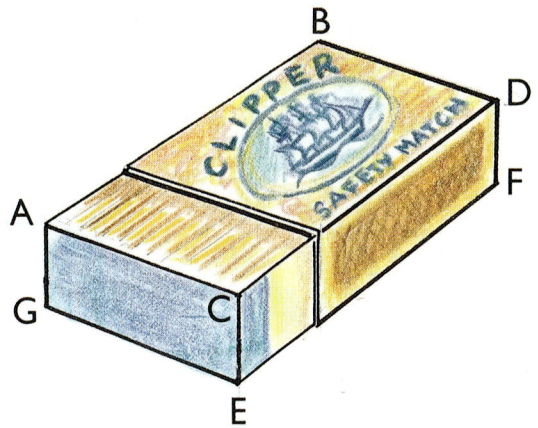

▶ Try May's idea by sliding the box open.

▶ Draw this line on a separate piece of paper. Make the line 15 cm long.

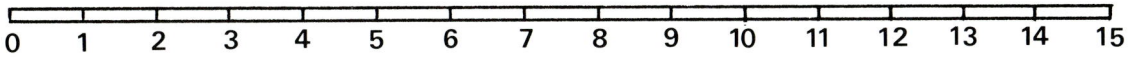

```
|0  1  2  3  4  5  6  7  8  9  10  11  12  13  14  15|
```

▶ Either use a set square or the corner of a cardboard box to draw two parallel lines which are 6 cm apart.

▶ Draw another line which is parallel to the first two.

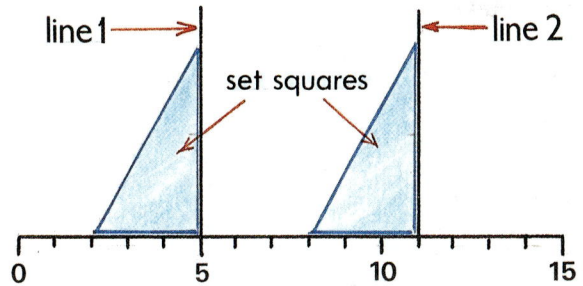

For example:

line 1 →   ← line 2

set squares

```
0        5        10        15
```

▶ Look around your home for parallel lines. There are lots of them on this clothes airer, and on this egg slicer.

▶ Make a list of the different places you can find them.

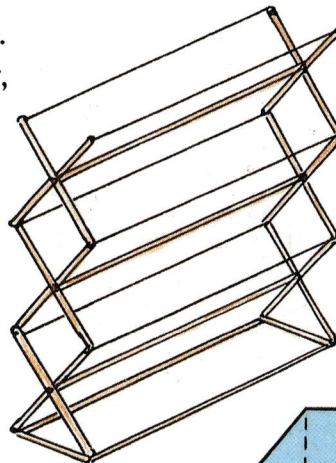

Please tell me how many pairs of parallel edges you can find on this cube.

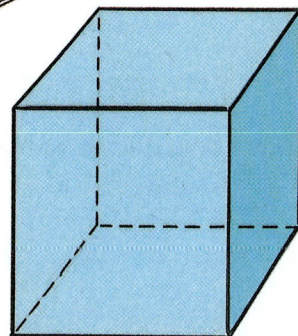

_____ pairs of parallel edges.

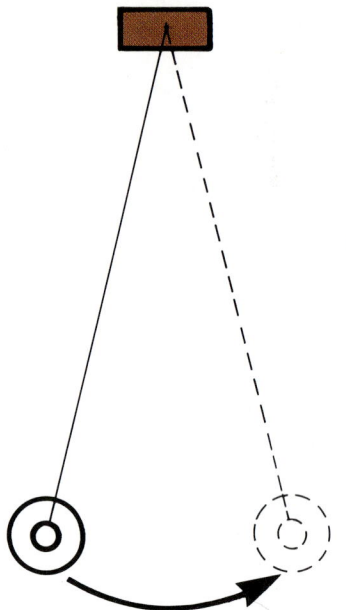

one swing of the pendulum

I made a pendulum like this with some thin string and a washer. I hung it on a hook. I wanted to make a second pendulum so I asked Gary to help me.

We had to find out what length of string (in cm) we needed for one swing to take one second. We started with a length of 30 cm, then we made a chart.

Length of string in cm	Time in secs	Number of swings
50	30 30 30 30 30	

▶ Here is the chart they started.

▶ Notice that they chose to count their swings over 30 seconds.

▶ Alter the length for more or less swings.

▶ Make a pendulum like May's and Gary's and see if you can find the length of string needed to make one swing take one second. Finish May's and Gary's chart.

▶ How many days are there in a million seconds?

▶ Use a calculator.

Cent means 100.
Kilo means 1000.
Do you know what mega means? It means 1 000 000 (one million).

I've never seen a million.

▶ Help Mark to see roughly what a million looks like. Think hard how to go about it.

You will need something small like rice, lentils or barley, but it would take a long time to <u>count</u> to a million.

Let's try weighing some rice.

Pat and Joe got some rice and some weighing scales. Then they made a chart to help them, like May and Gary with the pendulum!

Weight of rice in grams	Number of grains of rice
50 100	

▶ Ask a grown-up for some rice and the kitchen scales, then see if you can get some idea of a million. It will still take a long time!

Did you know:

It takes you about 6½ weeks to breathe a million times?

Answers

To Parents:

We have not provided *all* the answers here. We suggest that answers to be drawn in should be checked by you. In the case of activities where calculations are performed by your child, it would be good practice to get him/her to use a calculator to check the answers.

Unit No.	Answers
1	p.2 Parabola. Right angles. p.3 6 angles and 7 arms.
2	p.4 The draining board is not level. p.5 Spider travels vertically. 90°.
3	p.6 D–500, C–100, L–50. p.7 215 miles. 1970, 1980, 1990, 1911. I–IX–MLXVI. XXV–XII–MCMXC. 1615 At the end of a BBC programme it is in the © copyright line.
4	p.8 Stature ↔. p.9 Less than 1 fathom; 192cm, nearly 2m.
5	p.10 $26 + 45 + 25 = 96$ $54 + 38 + 50 = 142$. p.11 1. $20 \times 2 + 50 + 10$ or $2 \times 18 + 2 \times 19 + 2 \times 13$ or $20 \times 2 + 20 \times 2 + 20$ or $19 \times 3 + 13 + 2 \times 15$ and so on. 2. $60 + 60 + 60$. ($60 =$ treble 20) 3. $1 + 1 + 1$. 4. $2 \times 10 + 2 \times 10 + 2 \times 5$ or $2 \times 9 + 2 \times 11 + 2 \times 5$ or... 5. $2 \times 4 + 10 + 9$ or $2 \times 3 + 10 + 11$ or ... 6. $50 + 3 \times 20 + 2 \times 20$ or $3 \times 20 + 3 \times 18 + 2 \times 18$ or... Two ways, $1 + 2 \times 2$ or $3 + 2 \times 1$.
6	p.12 DIAMETER At the intersection of the two lines.
7	p.13 One twist: both appear to be on the inside and on the outside Hamid's loop: 1 large loop. p.14 $2 \rightarrow 1$; $3 \rightarrow 3$; $4 \rightarrow 6$; $5 \rightarrow 10$; $6 \rightarrow 15$; $7 \rightarrow 21$; $8 \rightarrow 28$. p.15 66 chords. $14 \rightarrow 4$ $15 \rightarrow 6$ $16 \rightarrow 8$. Cardioid.
8	p.16 South; east; south west; 3cm, 3km; 4cm, 4km; $5\frac{1}{2}$cm, $5\frac{1}{2}$km. May's journey – 17km. p.17 Crow distance – 5km. Real distance about 8km.

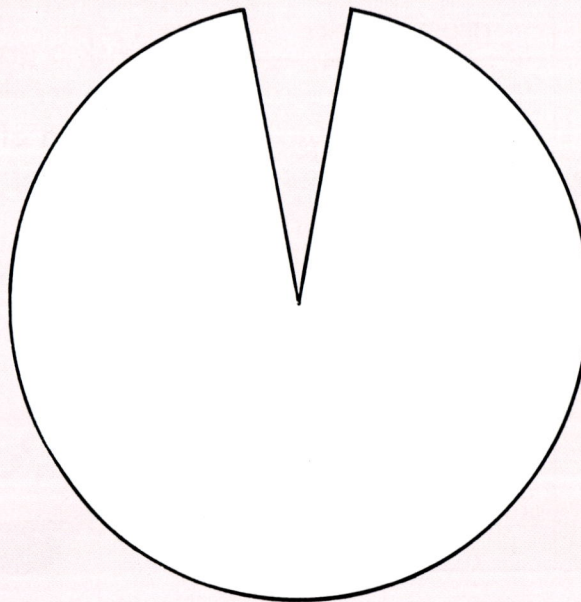

Unit No.	Answers
9	p.18 $\frac{1}{3} = 0.3333333$; $\frac{3}{4} = 0.75$; $\frac{1}{7} = 0.1428571$; $\frac{3}{7} = 0.4285714$. Exact: $\frac{1}{2} = 0.5$; $\frac{1}{4} = 0.25$; $\frac{3}{4} = 0.75$. p.19
10	p.20 333; 444; 555; 666; 777; 888; 999; and then magic disappears, 1110. $74 \times 3 = 222$; $74 \times 6 = 444$; $74 \times 9 = 666 \ldots$ p.21 3999996; 4999995; 6999993; 7999992. There are not enough digits on an ordinary calculator. 333333333; 444444444 . . . All 8s.
11	p.22
12	p.23 Circle has an infinite number. p.24 $10 \times 10 \times 10$; 1000 cubic cm = 1 litre p.25 1, 3, 8 litres. Beaker usually about 25cc. 7 bottles and 100cc left. 200 glasses.
13	p.26 £4.20 per week. £218.40 per year. £218. p.27 75g per week; 3900 in 1 year. 3750g; 150g. 4 cartons – 1kg. About 16 cartons or 4kg.
14	p.28 ART RAT TAR ATR RTA TRA. I II III IV II I III IV III II I IV IV I II III I II IV III II I IV III III II IV II IV I III II I III II IV II III I IV III II I IV IV II I III I III IV II II III IV I III II IV I IV II III I I IV II III II IV I III III IV I II IV III I II I IV III II II IV III I III IV II I IV III II I. p.29 123 132 213 231 321 312 Could be 132 or 312. 312. 4, 3, 2, 1 ways. $41 \times 32 = 1312$.
15	p.30 $\frac{2}{6}$ $\frac{3}{9}$ $\frac{4}{12}$ $\frac{5}{15}$ $\frac{6}{18}$ $\frac{7}{21}$ $\frac{8}{24}$ $\frac{9}{27}$ $\frac{10}{30}$. $\frac{2}{10}$ $\frac{3}{15}$ $\frac{4}{20}$ $\frac{5}{25}$ $\frac{6}{30}$ $\frac{7}{35}$ $\frac{8}{40}$ $\frac{9}{45}$ $\frac{10}{50}$. $\frac{2}{20}$ $\frac{3}{30}$ $\frac{4}{40}$ $\frac{5}{50}$ $\frac{6}{60}$ $\frac{7}{70}$ $\frac{8}{80}$ $\frac{9}{90}$ $\frac{10}{100}$. p.31 0.5; 0.05; 0.01; 0.2; 0.1. $\frac{1}{2} \rightarrow 0.50$; $\frac{1}{4} \rightarrow 0.25$; $\frac{1}{10} \rightarrow 0.10$; $\frac{1}{100} \rightarrow 0.01$; $\frac{1}{20} \rightarrow 0.05$.

Unit No.	Answers
16	p.32 No; Yes; No; Yes; No.
	p.33 Yes. Start where an odd number of paths meet.
	A 1 4 No D 2 2 Yes
	B 4 2 Yes E 0 8 No
	C 2 4 No F 3 2 Yes.
17	p.35 12 pairs are easy to see but there are 18 pairs.
18	p.36 11 days.